Neil deGrasse

Neil deGrasse Tyson was born October 5, 1958, the same week NASA was founded. He was born in the borough of Manhattan in New York, New York. His family lived in the Bronx. He was born to Sunchita Maria Feliciano Tyson and Cyril deGrasse Tyson. His mother was a gerontologist for the United States Department of Health, Education, and Welfare, while his father was a sociologist. He also worked as Mayor John Lindsay's human resource commissioner and was the first director for Harlem Youth Opportunities Limited, an organization dedicated to increasing educational and employment opportunities. In addition to Neil, Sunchita and Cyril had two other children, Stephen and Lynn; Tyson is the middle child.

Tyson spent his childhood in the Bronx, first in the Castle Hill neighborhood and then in Riverdale. He was educated in the borough's public schools, including P.S. 36, P.S. 81, and Riverdale Kingsbridge Academy. He attended high school at The Bronx High School of Science, where he was captain of the wrestling team and editor-in-chief of the Physical Science Journal. His describes his high school persona as "a nerd who could kick your butt." He also attended astronomy classes at the American Museum of Natural History's Hayden Planetarium, which is where his interest in astronomy was first piqued by a visit at the age of 9. Dr. Mark Chartrand III, who was then director of the planetarium, was an early role model for Tyson. Particularly influential was Chartrand's instruction style, which mixed teaching with humor.

So taken was Tyson with astronomy that attended astronomy camp in the Mojave Desert when he was 14 and began giving lectures on the subject at City University of New York a year later, when he was 15. Legendary astronomer Carl Sagan, who was on the faculty at Cornell University, tried to recruit Tyson for the university, even writing him a personal letter and giving him a tour of the campus. Contrary to somewhat popular belief, this would be only one of four times Sagan and Tyson met in person. However, Sagan's kindness inspired Tyson and he has credited the late astronomer with influencing how Tyson treats others.

Despite the push from Cornell, ultimately, though, Tyson

had his heart set on attending Harvard University. The Ivy League school had produced many prominent astrophysicists, which was what Tyson aspired to be. He was accepted and majored in physics. While at Harvard, he lived at Currier House. He took up crew, but went back to wrestling, in which he lettered during his senior year. He also joined a student dance group.

After earning an AB degree in physics at Harvard in 1980, Tyson went on to the University of Texas at Austin. As at Harvard, while in Texas, Tyson was active in athletics and dance. With UT's dance team, he won a gold medal at a national Latin ballroom dance competition. He briefly considered joining some of his male dance teammates who earned extra money performing as strippers. After catching one of their performances, in which his teammates came out in flaming costumes, to the strains of Jerry Lee Lewis's "Great Balls of Fire," he told NPR that he decided to become a math tutor, instead. He also wrote a column for the school's astronomy magazine *StarDate*. He would later use his material from the magazine in his first book, 1989's *Merlin's Tour of the Universe*, in which a fictional visitor from another planet mines his friendships with historical figures to answer questions about astronomy. Merlin continued his adventures in the 1998 sequel *Just Visiting This Planet: Merlin Answers More Questions about Everything under the Sun, Moon, and Stars.*

Tyson earned an MA degree in astrophysics at UT in 1983, but was unable to complete his doctorate. He admits that he did not devote enough time to research while in Austin and his dissertation committee was dissolved, effectively ending his time there. While his academic career was ultimately unsuccessful at Austin, he did take a relativity class there where he met Alice Young, whom he would later marry in 1988. They have had two children, Miranda (named after the moon of Uranus), who was born around 1996, and Travis, who was born around 2001.

After leaving UT, Tyson took a job at the University of Maryland in 1986 and lectured in astronomy there for a year. Even in his earliest forays into teaching, Tyson's instructional style, which blends humor and pop culture with real facts, was evident. In 1988, he was accepted into Columbia University's astronomy graduate program, where he earned an Mphil in astrophysics in 1989, as well as his PhD in 1991. His thesis was "A study of the abundance distributions along the minor axis of the

Galactic bulge." His supervisor at Columbia was Professor R. Michael Rich, who was able to secure funding for Tyson's research from NASA and the ARCS Foundation, the latter of which is devoted to funding graduate and undergraduate students in the STEM (science, technology, engineering, and mathematics) fields. With the funding, not only was Tyson able to hire students to help with the minutiae of data, but he was also able to travel to international conferences. As part of his thesis study, he made telescopic observations in Chile at the Cerro Tololo Inter-American Observatory for the Calán/Tololo Supernova Survey, which aided in the observatory's study of Type Ia supernovae. The information gathered by the observatory was used to refine the Hubble constant's measurement and led to the discovery in 1988 of dark matter.

Upon graduating from Columbia, Tyson then went on to Princeton, where he served as a postdoctoral research associate. While still at Princeton, he formally joined the staff of the Hayden Planetarium as a scientist. That same year, he wrote his second book, *Universe Down to Earth*, an introduction to natural science with an emphasis on astronomy. He became the acting director a year later in 1995. That same year he began writing the "Universe" column for *Natural History* magazine, which was run by the museum until the magazine was sold in 2002. Tyson became the official director of the planetarium a year after that.

As director, he brought on more research scientists and oversaw an ambitious $210 million renovation of the planetarium and its programs. The original planetarium was demolished and its place was built The Frederick Phineas and Sandra Priest Rose Center for Earth and Space, named for a donor family. The Rose Center, as it's known, is now a six-story glass cube with the new Hayden Planetarium's sphere "floating" in the middle. The bottom half of the sphere is the Big Bang Theater, which shows a 4-minute film that explains the formation of the universe. The top half of the sphere, the Star Theater, is the traditional planetarium theater. It uses a Zeiss Star Projector to project current astrophysical conditions, as well as other star shows in high-definition full-dome video. The sphere is wrapped by the Heilbrun Cosmic Pathway, which depicts the history of the universe and leads visitors to other related sections of the museum, like the Hall of Planet Earth. The Rose Center and the Hayden

Planetarium reopened in February 2000.

Around the time that the Center was opened, Tyson released two more books. The first was *One Universe: At Home in the Cosmos*, which he cowrote with Robert Irion and Charles Liu. Like Tyson's previous work, this book was an effort to make cosmic science more accessible to the general public. It features over 400 color photographs, which the authors use, along with everyday examples, to explain concepts that can be complicated. For example, they use an image of ladybugs on a balloon to describe the way that galaxies move and universes expand. The second book is *Cosmic Horizons: Astronomy at the Cutting Edge*, a collection of essays by astronomers for which Tyson served as an editor.

Tyson also started becoming more well-known around the time that the Center opened. In 2000, as part of their "Sexiest Man Alive" issue, *People* magazine named him the "Sexiest Astrophysicist Alive." (The "Sexiest Man Alive" overall that year was Brad Pitt.) In 2001, he was appointed to the Commission on the Future of the United States Aerospace Industry by President George W. Bush. That same year, he was a witness to the

September 11 attacks, as he lived near the World Trade Center. He wrote a widely-circulated e-mail about what he witnessed, saying in part, "How naive I was to believe that the world is fundamentally different from that of our ancestors, whose lives were changed by bearing witness to the 20th century's vilest acts of war." He also filmed footage that was included in the 2008 documentary *102 Minutes That Changed America*. An asteroid was also named for him that year. In a special edition of *Natural History* magazine released as a book called *City of Stars: A New Yorker's Guide to the Cosmos* in 2002, he shared the term "Manhattanhenge," which he had coined in 1996 to describe the twice-yearly time when the setting sun aligns with the east-west streets of Manhattan's grid. This phenomenon is also sometimes called the Manhattan Solstice, as it depends on the date of the summer solstice. The original term refers, of course, to England's Stonehenge monument, which was built to align with the rising sun during the summer solstice.

In 2003, Tyson released his 12-part lecture series *My Favorite Universe* in book form. The following year, President Bush appointed Tyson to the President's Commission on

Implementation of United States Space Exploration Policy, also known as "Moon, Mars, and Beyond." Around this time he was also awarded the NASA Distinguished Public Service Medal, NASA's highest civilian honor. He also released two more books in 2004, including *Origins: Fourteen Billion Years of Cosmic Evolution,* which was a companion book to the miniseries he made for PBS's Nova series called *Origins.* It was cowritten with Daniel Goldsmith. He also released *The Sky Is Not the Limit: Adventures of an Urban Astrophysicist.* In 2006, a Youtube user uploaded a talk between Tyson and biologist Richard Dawkins that served as an introduction to Tyson for many. The following year, a Neil deGrasse Tyson fanpage was created on Facebook.

One of the most controversial issues with which Tyson has been associated is the reclassification of Pluto. It began when the new planetarium organized an exhibit that depicted all bodies of the solar system. As Tyson intended, bodies were grouped with like bodies. Because of that, Pluto was not listed with the planets, but instead with objects of the Kuiper belt, a ring-shaped mass of gas just beyond Neptune that is home to Pluto and other dwarf planets. The planetarium, and Tyson in particular, received piles of mail from irate Pluto fans, many of them children. He wrote in The Sky Is Not the Limit, "I knew Pluto was popular among elementary schoolkids, but I had no idea they would mobilize into a 'Save Pluto' campaign. I now have a drawer full of hate letters from hundreds of elementary schoolchildren (with supportive cover letters from their science teachers) pleading with me to reverse my stance on Pluto." This was six years before Pluto would officially be reclassified as a dwarf planet by the International Astronomical Union. Tyson wrote about the controversy in 2009's *The Pluto Files: The Rise and Fall of America's Favorite Planet.* He theorized reasons that the decision had been upsetting to people who were sentimentally attached to the idea of Pluto as a planet. These reasons included cultural aspects like Mickey Mouse naming his dog after the space body and the fact that Pluto was the only one of the planets that had been discovered by an American astronomer, Clyde Tombaugh. Still, Tyson maintains that it was not him who made the ultimate decision. As he puts it, he did not "kill" Pluto as a planet: "All I did was drive the getaway car."

The Pluto controversy was also a popular topic for Tyson's

television appearances. He became a frequent guest on shows like Comedy Central's programs *The Colbert Report* and *The Daily Show*. On the latter show, he famously pointed out that the globe in *The Daily Show*'s intro was spinning in the wrong direction and once solved a Rubik's Cube while sitting in the green room, the television show's waiting room. Tyson has spoken before about how obsessed he became with solving the Rubik's Cube when it was first released. Tyson appeared on The Daily Show to promote books like 2007's *Death By Black Hole: And Other Cosmic Quandaries*. On *The Colbert Report*, host Stephen Colbert referred to Tyson as his BFF ("Best Friend Physicist").

Tyson has also been a guest on other television programs, including *Late Night with Conan O'Brien, The Tonight Show with Jay Leno, Late Night with Jimmy Fallon, Real Time with Bill Maher*, and news programs like *The Rachel Maddow Show* and *BBC Horizon*. He has also been a lifeline choice on *Who Wants to Be a Millionaire?* He has also made frequent appearances on the radio. He began his own radio show in 2009. It is called StarTalk and his first co-host was comedian Lynne Koplitz. It was first syndicated in Los Angeles (on KTLK AM) and in Washington, DC (on WHFS) on Sunday afternoons. It ran for just over three months in its original run. Tyson rebooted the program in 2010 with new co-hosts Chuck Nice and Leighann Lord, both comedians. Other comedians who have served as co-hosts include Eugene Mirman, John Oliver, and Kristen Schaal. The show includes guests who are fellow scientists and celebrities like Buzz Aldrin, George Takei, and Joan Rivers. Besides discussions with guests, the show features a segment called "Cosmic Queries," in which Tyson and others answer listener-submitted questions. Unlike its original run, it is no longer limited to terrestrial radio and is instead available in podcast form. In 2015, the program began running as *Star Talk*, a late night talk show on the National Geographic Channel. It follows a similar format to the podcast, where Tyson interviews celebrities about the ways in which their lives have intersected with science. All television episodes are available in audio-only versions on the podcast site. In its first season, the television program was nominated for an Emmy for "Best Informational Programming."

In addition to his own radio show, Tyson has appeared on NPR's quiz show *Wait Wait...Don't Tell Me!* He has also appeared on other radio shows, like Philadelphia's *Preston and Steve* and satellite radio programs like SiriusXM's *The Opie and Anthony Show*. He is also a frequent visitor to other podcasts. He has been a guest on podcasts like *The Skeptics' Guide to the Universe, Radiolab, Skepticality,* and *The Joe Rogan Experience.*

His appearance on skeptic-related podcasts is in keeping with his own personal beliefs, which run toward skepticism. Tyson is careful to respect the beliefs of others, while famously saying that "The good thing about science is that it's true whether or not you believe in it." He and noted skeptic James Randi co-delivered a lecture called *Skepticism* at the 93rd International Convention of the Phi Theta Kappa International Honor Society in 2011. Tyson has also been the keynote speaker at The Amazing Meeting, the conference the James Randi Educational Foundation hosts. Another program relating to skepticism that has featured Tyson as a guest is the podcast *Rationally Speaking*. Tyson used a transcript of his appearance on the show as a chapter in his 2012 book *Space Chronicles: Facing the Ultimate Frontier*, which is a collection of his previous work on NASA and the future of space travel. However, despite his many appearances on skeptic-related podcasts and at conferences, Tyson has bristled at the perception that he is an atheist, which often goes hand in hand with skepticism. Tyson has even gone so far as to edit his own Wikipedia page, removing statements that describe him as an atheist and instead, writing that he is an agnostic. Nevertheless, he prefers to avoid discussing religion.

Besides his numerous appearances on television talk shows, Tyson has also appeared as himself in fictional media. He has appeared in episodes of *Stargate Atlantis* and *The Big Bang Theory*. In addition, footage of him was shown in the movie 2013 *Europa Report*, a found footage film purportedly about the first mission to Europa, a moon of Jupiter's.

Tyson took on his most prominent media role in 2014. He had hosted a spinoff of PBS's *Nova* series called *Nova ScienceNow* from 2006-2011, but in 2014, he revived Carl Sagan's old program *Cosmos: A Personal Voyage*. The original series is considered a ground-breaking documentary and was PBS's highest rated program until Ken Burns's documentary series *The Civil War*. The new series that Tyson hosted was called *Cosmos: A Spacetime Odyssey*. While the original series aired on PBS, the new version aired on Fox, with a repeat and extra material airing the following night on the National Geographic Channel. It was also rebroadcast internationally. The show has had one season, but there have been discussions about doing more.

The show followed the format of Sagan's series, with 13 episodes and elements such as the "Cosmic Calendar," a way to visualize the history of the universe. However, the new series obviously had updated scientific information and in addition, it used cutting-edge computer-generated imagery and animation to illustrate the concepts discussed. Sagan's widow Ann Druyan, who wrote for the original program, also wrote for the reboot. Another person who was influential in getting the series to air was Seth MacFarlane, who has and has had several shows on the Fox network, most notably *Family Guy*. He provided funding for the new *Cosmos*, as well as served as its executive producer. He was moved to invest in something worthwhile and chose *Cosmos* because he had enjoyed the program as a child and because, like Tyson, he is disappointed at the stagnancy of American space exploration.

That lack of progress is a frequent subject for Tyson. He has long argued for increasing funding to NASA and believes that one of the roadblocks to more funding is the public perception that NASA is already well-funded. He says that he has spoken to people who believe that NASA gets as much as a dime from every tax dollar, when in fact, their funding amounts to a half of a penny. He has urged Congress to double that, testifying before the United States Senate Science Committee, "Right now, NASA's annual budget is half a penny on your tax dollar. For twice that—a penny on a dollar—we can transform the country from a sullen, dispirited nation, weary of economic struggle, to one where it has reclaimed its 20th century birthright to dream of tomorrow." The Space Advocates, a nonprofit devoted to increasing funding to the American space program, was inspired by Tyson to start their Penny4NASA campaign to advocate for doubling the funding.

Funding for NASA is not Tyson's only passion, of course. The majority of his work that is not related to his own research is devoted to increasing public interest in science in general. He is tireless when it comes to interacting with the public. He maintains an active Twitter account, @neiltyson, where he's become known for sharing interesting scientific facts and debunking the importance of holidays as arbitrary. On that note, he was criticized on Twitter for a tweet he wrote about Isaac Newton's birthday ("On this day long ago, a child was born who, by age 30, would transform the world. Happy Birthday Isaac Newton b. Dec 25, 1642") that some felt was offensive to Christians. Tyson ended up later writing a note on his Facebook page, which he had since taken control of, explaining that he had meant nothing anti-Christian by the tweet.

Tyson also became involved in a debate with recording artist B.o.B., who began expressing his belief in January 2016 that the earth is flat. Tyson first tried to reason with the rapper, but B.o.B. refused to entertain Tyson's arguments. In fact, he ended up recording a "diss track" aimed at Tyson. Titled "Flatline," the song not only takes shots at Tyson, but also includes references to a number of conspiracy theories B.o.B. apparently espouses. These include popular conspiracy theories about Freemasons and Holocaust denial.

The rapper later removed the track from his Soundcloud account after it was criticized, including by the Anti-Defamation League. Tyson, along with his nephew, rapper Steve Tyson, recorded a response diss called "Flat to Fact." Tyson also appeared on Comedy Central's program *The Nightly Show with Larry Wilmore* to rebut the rapper, saying in part, "Small sections of large curved surfaces will always look flat to little creatures that crawl upon it...and by the way, this is called gravity," before dropping the mic.

Ironically, on the original *Cosmos,* Carl Sagan once debunked the popular myth that people in Christopher Columbus's lifetime thought that the earth was flat. He demonstrated how Eratosthenes, who died in 194 BC Greece, knew that the earth was round. In fact, Eratosthenes used that knowledge and measurements of the sun's position in different areas, to calculate the circumference of the planet.

Tyson, always a champion of better science education, often corrects bad science in pop culture. For example, he has been a three-time guest on the Youtube program CinemaSins, which catalogs film errors. Tyson has appeared on the program to discuss the movies *Gravity, Interstellar*, and *The Martian*. While he has not discussed the film *Titanic* on the show, he did notify director James Cameron that in the scene where Rose (Kate

Winslet) is floating in the water, the night sky above her is incorrect. Worse than that, according to Tyson, she's actually only looking at one half of the sky—it's a mirror reflection on the other side. According to Tyson, Cameron brushed him off when they met face-to-face, but later, Tyson was contacted by a member of Cameron's production team for the correct data and the shot was replaced for the movie's 2012 re-release.

As Tyson's fame has grown, he has become a pop-culture figure, as evidenced by his appearance on shows like *The Big Bang Theory*. He is frequently paired with fellow popular science figure Bill Nye. Tyson has also seen himself become a meme, as an image of him taken from a video where he's coincidentally discussing Isaac Newton was turned into a "rage comic," an image used to express a reaction. The image of Tyson used is a still shot when he was saying in the video, "That's my man, right there" about Newton. He has his hands up and a funny expression on his face. The image was often used "in a sarcastic manner to [respond to] boastful and arrogant statements," according to the website Know Your Meme. Although Tyson initially found being a meme "creepy," he grew to accept it.

This has not been Tyson's only appearance in cartoon form. On animated television programs, he has voiced himself and characters based on himself like the "planetarium narrator" on *Bojack Horseman*. He also voiced "Neil deBuck Weasel," a weasel character in the 2016 animated film *Ice Age: Collision Course*. He was also depicted in an issue of *Action Comics*. In issue #14 from January 2013, comic book Tyson locates Superman's home planet Krypton. Real life Tyson picked the constellation Corvus, which is Latin for "crow," as the location as a reference to Smallville's mascot, the Crows. In keeping with the Superman theme, Tyson also made an appearance in 2016's *Batman vs. Superman: Dawn of Justice*. That same year, he appeared on heavy metal band Avenged Sevenfold's album *The Stage* on the track "Exist" and in 2017, appeared on rapper Logic's album *ƎVERYBODY* on the track "AfricAryaN."

In addition to his frequent appearances on television and in film, Tyson also often gives guest lectures and keynote speeches, such as the one he gave at Massachusetts's Deerfield Academy in 2007 to mark the dedication of their new science building, the Koch Center. He has mentioned on an episode of his podcast

StarTalk that he donates all of his income from guest speeches. He also often interacts with the public. He has done multiple AMAs on the website Reddit, which are among some of the most popular AMAs of all time. AMA, which stands for "Ask Me Anything," is a post where Reddit users can post questions to a celebrities and other people, who then answer questions of their choice. Tyson's AMAs have covered everything from questions about science to personal questions, such as his favorite comedians. (Tyson listed 11 favorite comedians that included Richard Pryor, Eddie Murphy, and Jerry Seinfeld.)

In 2016, the 13th book featuring Tyson's work was published. Called *Welcome to the Universe: An Astrophysical Tour*, it was co-authored with Michael A. Strauss and J. Richard Gott. The book is based on the introductory astrophysics course they taught at Princeton and was published by the Princeton University Press. The book, like others Tyson has had a hand in writing, was well-received by critics and readers alike. Tyson followed that book with 2017's *Astrophysics for People in a Hurry*, which was adapted from the "Universe" column he wrote for *Natural History* magazine. Tyson made media appearances to promote the book, appearing on programs as diverse as the PBS staple *Charlie Rose* and Viceland's *Desus & Mero*. In addition to the books he's written and the columns in popular science magazines, Tyson has continued to write for industry-specific publications. These include *Astronomical Journal* and *Astrophysical Journal*.

Tyson has received a number of awards and other recognition beyond his reigning title as "Sexiest Astrophysicist Alive." He won a Medal of Excellence from Columbia University in 2001, his earliest award. That same year, he was named by *Crain's Magazine* as one of the Tech 100, one of New York's 100 most influential technology leaders. In 2004, *Essence* magazine named him one of the 50 Most Important African-Americans in Research Science. The following year, he won the Science Writing Award, given by the American Institute of Physics, for his work in *Natural History* magazine. He followed that in 2007 with the Klopsteg Memorial Award. The latter award is given each year to an outstanding physicist in memory of American physicist Paul E. Klopsteg. The award is given by the American Association of Physics Teachers and the recipient of the award is expected to give a presentation at the AAPT Summer Meeting on a topic of their choice. The topic must be relevant to current science and it must be accessible to laypeople. Tyson's topic was "Adventures in Science Literacy." Also in 2007, *Harvard Alumni* magazine named him as one of the Harvard 100: Most Influential and *Time* magazine chose him for the Time 100, their list of the most influential people in the world.

In 2008, *Discover* magazine continued in this vein, naming him one of the "10 Most Influential People in Science." For his work contributing to public awareness of American space programs, Tyson received the Douglas S. Morrow Public Outreach Award in 2009 from the Space Foundation. That same year, the American Humanist Organization, which is devoted to promoting Secular Humanism, a philosophy that advocates for personal responsibility and ethics without theistic beliefs ("Good without a God"), gave him their Isaac Asimov Science Award.

Tyson managed to go a few years without receiving further awards or honors until 2014, when he won the Critics' Choice Television Award for Best Reality Show Host for his work on Cosmos. He beat out Tom Bergeron, Carson Daly, Cat Deeley, Gordon Ramsay, and RuPaul. That year, he also won the Dunlap

Prize. The award, which is from the University of Toronto's Dunlap Institute for Astronomy & Astrophysics, was created to honor the "individual whose remarkable achievements resonate with the Dunlap's goals for excellence in astronomy and astrophysics." Tyson was the first recipient of the Prize. He appeared for the ceremony at the University and afterward, gave a guest lecture to a packed crowd in the University's Convocation Hall.

The following year, in 2015, the United States National Academy of Sciences awarded him the Public Welfare Medal, which is given "in recognition of distinguished contributions in the application of science to the public welfare." Tyson specifically was given the award "[F]or his extraordinary role in exciting the public about the wonders of science, from atoms to the Universe." He also won the Cosmos Award from the Planetary Society that year. The Planetary Society, which was founded by Carl Sagan among others, is devoted to knowing "our place in the cosmos." Tyson has served as the vice president, president, and chairman of the board of directors for the society. Currently, he is one of their advisors.

In addition to his many awards and honors, Tyson has been awarded a large number of honorary doctorates. His first was from York College of the City University of New York in 1997 and he has been awarded many since then. Some of the educational institutions that have given him honorary doctorates include schools with strong ties to the American space program, like Huntsville, Alabama's University of Alabama at Huntsville, whose science curricula were honed by German rocket engineer Wernher von Braun. Other schools who have awarded him honorary doctorates include Mount Holyoke College in South Hadley, Massachusetts, and New York City's Pace University.

Today, Tyson continues to live in Lower Manhattan with his wife and son Travis. He still serves as the first and only Frederick P. Rose Director of the Hayden Planetarium. He continues to write for magazines and other publications and will surely continue to write more books. He will also certainly make more television appearances, if not on a future tentative season of Cosmos, then on other programs. When he's not teaching science and advocating for his many pet causes, one of Tyson's other passions in life is gourmet food and wine. His wine collection is well-known and has been featured in publications like *Wine Spectator* magazine (May 2000) and *The World of Fine Wine* (Spring 2005).

Made in the USA
San Bernardino, CA
23 May 2018